POETRY PARADE

Written by Pamela Amick Klawitter
Illustrated by Beverly Armstrong

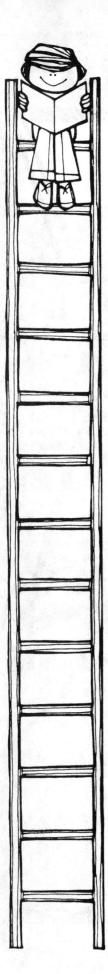

The Learning Works

Edited by Sherri M. Butterfield

The purchase of this book entitles the individual teacher to reproduce copies for use in the classroom.

The reproduction of any part for an entire school or school system or for commercial use is strictly prohibited.

No form of this work may be reproduced or transmitted or recorded without written permission from the publisher.

Contents

To the Teacher

This book is designed to help boys and girls in the fourth through the sixth grades have fun with poetry and discover on their own that poems come in all sizes and shapes to express many feelings and to fit many moods.

Poetry Parade is divided into four sections. The first section, entitled **Poems That Follow a Pattern**, contains simple, nonrhyming poems that follow a predetermined pattern or fill a prescribed shape. The second section, **Poems That Rhyme**, introduces four types of poetry that conform to various rhyme schemes. The third section, entitled **Miscellaneous Poems**, offers additional experiences in poetry writing and introduces students to such literary devices as alliteration, metaphor, onomatopoeia, and simile. The fourth section, **Poetry Projects**, which includes both a list of special projects and a mini-book, offers creative outlets for student-generated poems.

In using **Poetry Parade** with your class, there are several things to keep in mind. First, reading poetry aloud, talking about rhyme schemes, and having students clap or move in rhythm may make them more sensitive to these essential elements of poetry. Second, even though the book has been written to allow students to work independently, they will derive greater benefit from their study of poetry if they share what they have written and learned. For this reason, you should schedule periods for poetry sharing on a regular basis. During these periods, encourage students to read aloud the favorites they have found or written. Third, the poetry contract on page 35 will help you provide appropriate poetry experiences for all of your students while making allowances for their individual differences. In each contract category, the second choice is geared to the gifted learner.

Name _____

Five W's Poem

A **five w's poem** is a five-line nonrhyming poem designed to answer the following questions: Who? What? When? Where? Why?

Structure:

line 1—**Who** or what is the poem about?
line 2—**What** is he, she, or it doing?
line 3—**When** does this action take place?
line 4—**Where** does it take place?
line 5—**Why** does it take place?

Example:
The ducks
glide silently
from morning 'til night
across the still pond,
watching their reflections.

On your own: Write a five w's poem. Make sure it tells a story.

_____

_____

_____

_____

_____

Just for fun: Find an interesting picture in an old book, magazine, or calendar, and compose a five w's poem about it.

Name _____

Seasonal Haiku

A **haiku** is a three-line, unrhymed Japanese poem with lines of five, seven, and five syllables, respectively. Poems of this type are usually light and delicate in feeling and are often written about nature.

Structure:

line 1—five syllables
line 2—seven syllables
line 3—five syllables

Example: These haiku verses linked together tell a story of the changing seasons.

Tiny seed is dropped—
Tender shoots burst from within.
Green arms reach skyward.

Thirst-quenching rain falls.
Leaves bask in golden sunlight.
First buds pop open.

Glorious blossoms!
Shiny leaves wave; stem stands proud.
Mother Nature smiles.

A trace of color,
Lovely flower's end is near.
Faded blossoms fall.

On your own: Choose an element of nature that changes with the seasons, such as the sky, a tree, a flower, or a river. Write four haiku verses that describe this element over a period of time. Print your finished verses on page 7. On separate sheets of paper, create a picture to illustrate each verse. Consider working with watercolors or with brush and ink.

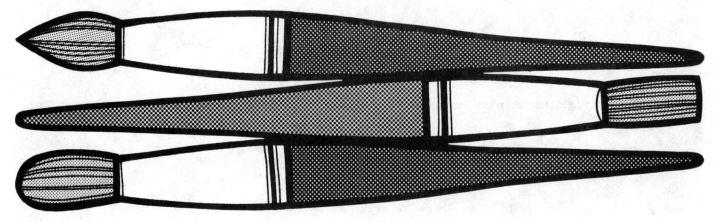

Name _____

Seasonal Haiku

_____

_____

_____

_____

_____

_____

_____

_____

_____

_____

_____

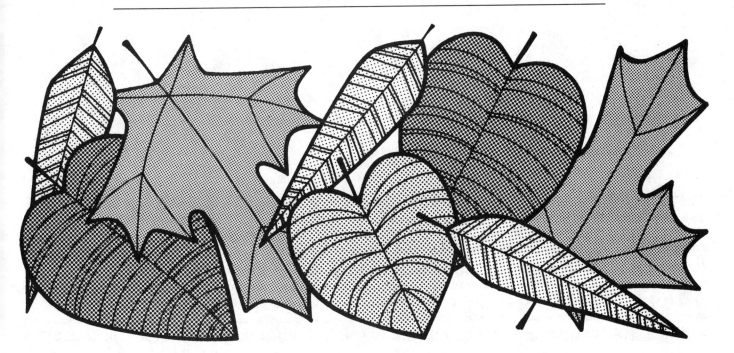

Name _____

Quinzaine

The English word **quinzaine** comes from the French word *quinze*, meaning fifteen. A quinzaine is an unrhymed verse of fifteen syllables. These syllables are distributed among three lines so that there are seven syllables in the first line, five in the second line, and three in the third line. The first line makes a statement. The next two lines ask a question relating to that statement.

Structure:

line 1—seven syllables
line 2—five syllables
line 3—three syllables

Examples:

Birds fly beneath darkened clouds.
Do they sense the storm
approaching?

Snow's white blanket covers all.
Will spring ever break
winter's hold?

On your own:

_____

_____

_____

_____

_____

_____

Name _____

Acrostic Poem

An **acrostic** is a piece of poetry or prose in which sets of letters taken in order form a word or phrase. An **acrostic poem** is a short verse in which each letter of the title is used as the initial letter for one line. In a poem of this kind, the lines need not rhyme.

Examples:

Swimming
Splashing
Water
In
My
Mouth
Is
No . . .
Gulp . . . fun!

Piano
Practice! Practice! Practice!
It's all my mother says.
As if more pounding will help the
Notes make sense,
Or turn the noise into music.

Skateboard
Skinned-up
Knees
And
Two sore
Elbows are the
Badges
Of
All
Real
Daredevils!

On your own: On the lines below, write an acrostic poem about a favorite hobby, sport, or pastime. To make the title and the first letter of each line stand out, print them in a color that is different from the one you use for the rest of the poem.

_____

_____

_____

_____

_____

_____

_____

_____

Name _____

Cinquain

A **cinquain** is a simple, five-line verse that follows a specific pattern.

Structure:

line 1—one word of two syllables (usually a noun that names the subject of the poem)

line 2—four syllables (often two two-syllable adjectives describing the noun in line 1)

line 3—six syllables (often three *-ing* words also describing the noun in line 1)

line 4—eight syllables (a phrase or sentence about the noun in line 1)

line 5—two syllables (a word or two that rename the noun in line 1)

Examples:

Earthworm—
Wiggly, slimy,
Creeping, slinking, searching—
Slithers silently on his way.
Slowpoke!

Sneakers—
Threadbare, worn-out,
Fading, shredding, reeking—
Ahh! Finally comfortable!
Old friends.

On your own: On the five lines below, write a cinquain.

_____

_____

_____

_____

_____

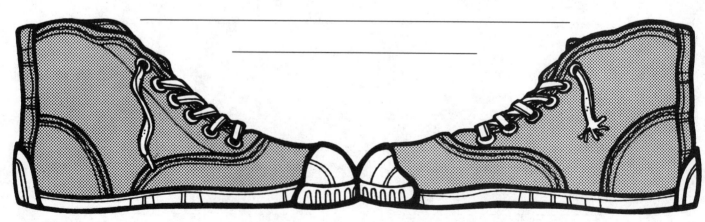

Name _____

Greetings!

Design a greeting card for a birthday or holiday, or simply to show someone special that you care. No matter what your theme or purpose, the cinquain is the perfect poetic form for such a project.

Example:

front   inside

On your own:

1. Fold a rectangular sheet of white paper in half.

2. Choose a subject for your poem. Many common names for relatives, such as mother, father, sister, brother, grandma, grandpa, uncle, and cousin, have two syllables and so are suitable to appear as the first line of a cinquain. You might also consider using two-syllable proper names or nicknames.

3. Carefully letter a greeting on the front of the card, and print your personalized cinquain on the inside. Center each line of your poem, and form and space the letters carefully.

4. Use colored pencils, crayons, marking pens, or paints to decorate the card.

5. Mail or hand-deliver your custom-created greeting.

Diamante

The French word **diamant** means "diamond." The French word **diamante** means "set with diamonds or other similar sparkling decoration." A **diamante** is a poem set, or written, in the shape of a diamond. Thus, it progresses from a short opening line through lines of increasing length to a single long line and back to a short line. This verse form has several recognized variations. For example, one type of five-line diamante is similar to the cinquain.

Structure:

line 1—your first name
line 2—two adjectives that describe you
line 3—three verbs that tell what you can do
line 4—four adjectives that tell how you act or feel
line 5—your name again or your nickname

Example:

Sarah
Curious, athletic
Explore, dance, learn
Confident, easy-going, good-humored, optimistic
Sarah

On your own: On the lines below, write a diamante that tells about you.

_____

_____

_____

_____

_____

GENTLE · SMART · HONEST
BRAVE · HELPFUL · SILLY
ACTIVE · HAPPY · CARING

Diamante

The most common form of diamante is the seven-line version. This form is written about two contrasting or opposite subjects and makes a comparison between them by moving from one to the other.

Structure:

line 1—one noun that names the first subject of the diamante
line 2—two adjectives that describe the first subject
line 3—three -*ing* words that are related to the first subject
line 4—four nouns, the first two related to the first subject (named in line 1) and the second two related to the second subject (named in line 7)
line 5—three -*ing* words that are related to the second subject
line 6—two adjectives that describe the second subject
line 7—one noun that names the second subject of the diamante

Example:

Egg
Tiny, blue
Rocking, cracking, exploding
Nest, shell, beak, foot
Squawking, gazing, shivering
Wide-eyed, feathery
Bird

On your own: On the lines below, write a diamante in which you make a comparison between two opposite or contrasting objects or ideas.

_____

_____

_____

_____

_____

_____

_____

fire-ice acorn-oak war-peace

Name _____

Wish Poem

Have you ever wished that you could be someone other than yourself, doing something other than what you usually do, for just one day? Here's your chance to express that wish in a poem. A **wish poem** is a slightly altered version of the cinquain in which the poet expresses his or her wish to be someone else somewhere else doing something else.

Structure:

line 1—is the opening statement, *I wish I were*
line 2—tells **who** you would like to be
line 3—tells **where** you would like to be
line 4—often begins with an *-ing* word and tells **what** you would like to be doing
line 5—is an adverb that tells **how** you would do it

Example:

I wish I were
An astronaut
Soaring high above the earth
Blazing new trails
Proudly.

I wish I were
Mary Lou Retton
Poised on the balance beam
Ready to perform
Perfectly.

On your own: First, think about who you would like to be. Then, on the lines below, write a wish poem in which you tell who you would like to be, where you would like to be, what you would like to be doing, and how you would do it.

_____

_____

_____

_____

_____

Just for fun: On a separate sheet of paper, illustrate your poem by drawing a picture of yourself in your new role.

Name _____

Pick a Pair

A **couplet** is a two-line poem. While the length of the lines may vary from one couplet to the next, the lines within a couplet always rhyme.

Examples:

I have so very many baseball cards
I measure my collection by the yards

   The wooden horse rocks to and fro
   With no important place to go.

   The wide-eyed frog laughed and joked
   Until one day he simply croaked.

On your own: Pick a pair of rhyming words from the box and use them to write a couplet on the lines below.

baboon - balloon	pest - test	shark - spark
earthquake - mistake	pickle - nickel	skate - gate
gnu - flu	reach - beach	smoke - choke
goat - quote	school - cool	sneeze - fleas
knot - spot	self - shelf	under - wonder

_____

_____

Name _____

Triangular Triplet

A **triangular triplet** is a three-line rhyming verse whose lines are nearly equal in length and can be read in any order.

Example:

On your own: Write the three lines of a triangular triplet along the sides of the equilateral triangle below.

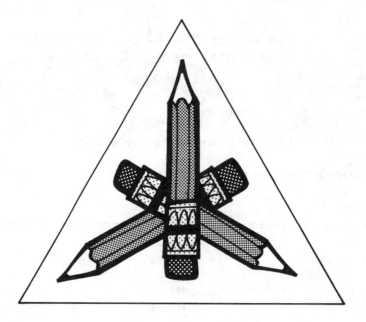

Just for fun: Draw a large equilateral triangle on white paper. Print this triplet or another one you have written along the sides of this large triangle. Illustrate the triplet inside the triangle.

Name _____

Who's Who Clerihew

The **clerihew** gets its name from Edmund Clerihew Bentley (1875-1956), the English writer of detective stories who originated this verse form. A clerihew is a comical four-line poem about a person. This mini-biography consists of two rhyming couplets, and the first line ends with the person's name.

Example:

"I'm quite surprised," said Henry Ford.
"My greatest feat has been ignored!
The car's no big deal. Clever man that I am,
I have invented the traffic jam!"

On your own: On the lines below, write two clerihews, one about a famous person you have studied and one about someone you know.

_____

_____

_____

_____

_____

_____

_____

_____

Just for fun: Make a clerihew time line for your classroom. Collect clerihews about famous people from your classmates. Print or type each clerihew on a card. Label each card with the first and last names of the person described and with his or her birth and death dates. Display the cards in chronological order on a classroom bulletin board or wall.

Name _____

Triolet

A **triolet** is a short, eight-line French verse form that gets its name from the fact that the first line appears three times, as lines 1, 4, and 7. Because the second line is repeated as the eighth, lines 2 and 8 are also identical. The rhyme scheme of the triolet is ABaAabAB.

Example:

Mary Margaret McCoy
She's my best friend.
Her company I enjoy,
Mary Margaret McCoy.
We need no game or toy;
Her imagination knows no end.
Mary Margaret McCoy
She's my best friend.

On your own: On the lines below, write a triolet about someone you know or about something you like.

_____

_____

_____

_____

_____

_____

_____

Just for fun: The prefix *tri-* means "three." When used as part of a larger word, it may mean "three elements, parts, or times." This prefix is present in the word **triplet**, which names a unit of verse. How many lines does a triplet contain?

Name _____

Comparisons

Poets often create pictures with words by comparing one thing with another. In this way, they help the readers of their poems see similarities between things in new and different ways. When a poet uses the word *like* or *as* in a comparison, he or she is writing a **simile**.

Examples:

*The star glittered **like** a diamond.*

*The sunset was **as** red **as** fire.*

When a poet compares two things by equating one with the other or by saying that one thing *is* another, he or she is writing a **metaphor**.

Examples:

His anger was an unexploded bomb waiting to go off.

The cat's eyes were burning embers in the coal-black night.

On your own: On the lines below, write two similes and two metaphors.

Similes

_____

_____

Metaphors

_____

_____

Just for fun: Write and illustrate a poem based on one of the similes or metaphors you created.

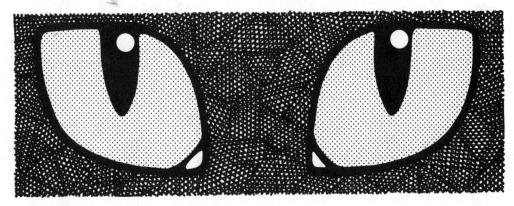

Name _____

The Most Amazing Thing

Poets often write about their unusual experiences. A **most-amazing-thing-I've-ever-seen poem** is a one-sentence poem in which the author paints a word picture of something amazing he or she has actually seen. In this type of poem, the words are not written in long lines across a page. Instead, they are divided into small groups and arranged in short lines that form an interesting or pleasing pattern. Poems of this sort usually begin with the words "The most amazing thing I've ever seen." As a variation, you may wish to substitute the words *funniest, oddest, ugliest,* or *most beautiful* for *most amazing.*

Examples:

The most amazing thing
I've ever seen
was a death-defying flower
poking its delicate petals
through the volcanic ash
on
Mount St. Helens.

The most beautiful thing
I've ever seen
was a
sun-drenched beach
after a storm.

On your own: Follow these examples to write a poem of this type on the lines below.

_____

_____

_____

_____

_____

_____

_____

Name _____

Parody

A **parody** is a poem, story, or song in which an author's style is closely imitated for comic effect. Which nursery rhymes are being parodied in the following examples?

Examples:

Little Miss Crocker
Sat in her rocker
Eating a burger and fries.
Along came a bee
And perched on her knee,
Giving her quite a surprise!

Zack, be clumsy.
Zack, be slow.
Zack tripped over his own big toe!

On your own: Write a parody of one of the following nursery rhymes: Jack and Jill, Little Jack Horner, Humpty Dumpty, Little Bo Peep, Peter Piper, Mary Had a Little Lamb, or Hickory Dickory Dock.

Just for fun: Draw a cartoon character to accompany your nursery rhyme parody.

Name _____

Cut-and-Paste Poem

Sometimes, simple combinations of words can become a form of poetry when they are arranged in a way that enhances their meaning and is pleasing to the eye. In **cut-and-paste poems**, words and phrases cut from print media are especially arranged to express a feeling or to make a statement. Poems of this kind come in all lengths and need not necessarily conform to a particular line pattern or rhyme scheme.

Example:

On your own: Search through old newspapers and magazines for interesting words and phrases. Cut out the ones that appeal to you. Once you have a variety, place several of them on a sheet of white drawing paper. Arrange and rearrange them until you are pleased with the result. When you are satisfied, glue the words and phrases in place on the paper. Cut out and glue a title above your cut-and-paste poem or print one using a black broad-tipped marking pen.

Name _____

More Cut-and-Paste Poetry

This version of a cut-and-paste poem starts with a picture cut from a magazine, calendar, or catalog. Choose a full-page illustration that interests you. Trim it and glue it on colored paper. From old magazines or newspapers, cut words and phrases that describe the mood or action depicted in the picture. Arrange these words and phrases on top of the picture. When you are satisfied with your arrangement, glue the words and phrases in place.

Example:

Name _____

Thesaurus? Of Course!

To write interesting poetry or prose, you must have a storehouse of colorful, descriptive words and phrases at your disposal. One way to stretch your vocabulary is by using a thesaurus. A **thesaurus** is a book in which many of the words of a language are listed in alphabetical order, and synonyms are given for them.

On your own: Look up these common words in a thesaurus. Below each word list the most unusual synonyms you find for it.

big	*cold*	*pretty*
_____	_____	_____
_____	_____	_____
_____	_____	_____
_____	_____	_____

barbigerous · leucodermatous · grandiloquent
mucilaginous · blithesome · pachydermatous
obstreperous · effervescent · megalomaniacal

You can practice using some of the new words you have found in the thesaurus by substituting them for the "old" words in familiar song lyrics or nursery rhymes. For example, you might rewrite *Three blind mice* to be *A trio of sightless rodents*. Following this example, rewrite the nursery rhyme lines below by substituting less familiar synonyms for some of the more familiar words in them.

Little Bo-peep has lost her sheep

_____

This little pig went to market

_____

Name _____

In Other Words

Once you have become familiar with the thesaurus, put it to use. Choose a poem and rewrite both the title and the text on the lines below, substituting synonyms for many of the key words. This task will be more difficult but the results will be more satisfying if you try to retain the rhythm, rhyme scheme, mood, and/or meaning that characterize the original poem on which your new one is based. When you have finished rewriting, challenge a friend to read what you have written and to identify the original poem.

_____

_____

_____

_____

_____

_____

_____

_____

_____

_____

_____

_____

tan cow

beige bovine

Name _____

Window Poem

Many would-be authors never write because they cannot think of a topic for their poetry or prose. Evidently, they do not realize that a poem or story is waiting right outside the nearest window. **Window poem** is a simple name given to verses that are inspired by the picture caught within a window frame.

Example:

> *A gray sky*
> *holds the threat of rain.*
> *Birds flutter to safety.*
> *Raindrops chase the children indoors.*
> *The playground stands empty and alone.*

On your own: Sit for a few minutes and gaze out the window. What do you see—a peaceful countryside, a noisy street, a busy neighborhood playground, a vacant lot, a neighbor's house? What is going on? What is the weather like? On the lines below, jot down your impressions. Then, on a separate sheet of paper, write a window poem based on them.

_____

_____

_____

_____

_____

_____

_____

Just for fun: Use crayons, marking pens, or watercolors to create a picture of the scene you have described in your window poem.

Name _____

Contrast Poem

A **contrast poem** has two parts that show different sides, or aspects, of the same subject.

Examples:

Signs of Spring

Rusty cans
lie among
broken bottles and
hamburger wrappers.

A blade of grass
pokes through the rubbish,
and tiny yellow flowers
lift their heads.

Dog Days

The frisky puppy
barks and jumps
as he chases the butterfly.

The old dog
rests on the porch,
preferring to watch.

On your own: First, choose a topic and think of two different ways of looking at it. Then, on the lines below, write a two-part poem about this topic. Present one point of view in the first part and a contrasting point of view in the second part. Each part, or **stanza**, should have the same number of lines, but the lines need not rhyme.

_____

_____

_____

_____

_____

_____

_____

_____

Name _____

Creepy-Crawlies

Creepy-crawlies are poems written about the tiny worlds of bustling activity that go unnoticed in backyards and on playgrounds. You may be surprised at what is taking place beneath your feet if you stop and look carefully enough to get an ant's-eye view.

Example:

Nine to Five

Three ants scurry off to work,
Dodging twigs and blades of grass.
One pauses to rest in the shade of a dandelion umbrella.
Another struggles as he drags his prey homeward.
The third keeps watch from atop a pebble tower.
As sundown signals the end of the workday,
They disappear, one by one, into a tiny sand volcano.

On your own:

1. Cut a yard-long piece of brightly colored yarn and tie the ends together to form a loop.
2. Choose a quiet outdoor spot where you won't be disturbed.
3. Use your yarn loop to outline an area you want to examine more closely.
4. Watch the activity inside your yarn loop very carefully. What do you see?
5. Make notes in which you list everything that happens inside your loop.
6. Use your notes to write a creepy-crawly.
7. Copy your finished poem inside the border on page 29.
8. In the space below the poem, create an appropriate illustration for it.

Name _____

_____

_____

_____

_____

_____

_____

_____

_____

_____

_____

_____

By _____

Name _____

Let's Get Lyrical

Songwriters are poets who write verses to go with music. The words, or **lyrics**, of their poems can be sung to the accompaniment of musical instruments.

On your own: Read the lyrics of one of your favorite songs or listen to a recording of them. On the lines below, write the title of this song and at least one verse of its lyrics. As you do so, notice the rhyme scheme and the line length used for these lyrics. What story do the lyrics tell? On a separate sheet of paper, write a new verse for the song which adds to or changes this story in some way.

_____

_____

_____

_____

_____

_____

_____

_____

_____

_____

_____

_____

_____

_____

_____

Name _____

Say It Again!

A **say-it-again poem** is based on a repeated word or phrase. It may have any number of lines, and the lines do not need to rhyme.

Example:

Just Now I . . .

Just now I turned off my alarm clock.
Just now I jumped out of bed.
Just now I quickly dressed.
Just now I gulped down my breakfast.
Just now I grabbed my books.
Just now I ran out the door and headed for school.
Just now I remembered . . . it's Saturday!

On your own: First, choose a word or phrase to serve as the title of a say-it-again poem and as the beginning of each line in the poem. Then, use this word or phrase to write a poem on the lines below.

_____

_____

_____

_____

_____

_____

_____

_____

_____

_____

_____

Name _____

Alliteration

Alliteration is the repetition of a sound within a word, line, or phrase. A familiar use of this device is in tongue twisters and nursery rhymes. For example, in the line *She sells seashells down by the seashore*, the *s* is repeated; and in the line *Peter Piper picked a peck of pickled peppers*, the *p* is repeated. Poets often use alliteration to add humor to their poetry or to create special effects.

On your own: Write an alliterative phrase that follows the pattern in the example below.

Five
Fat
Fishermen
Found
Four
Frisky
Frogs.

Write a couplet in which you use alliteration for comic effect.

_____

_____

Six snails slid slowly south.

Name _____

Echoic Poems

The word **echoic** is an adjective made from the more familiar word **echo**. It means "formed in imitation of some natural sound." Thus, **echoic words** are words we have made up to imitate, or echo, the sounds we hear. Some examples of echoic words are *bow-wow, buzz, fizz, gurgle, hiss, meow, moo, sizzle, splat,* and *swish*. When words of this type are used in a poem, it is called an **echoic poem**. The use in poetry or prose of words whose sounds suggest their sense, or meaning, is called **onomatopoeia**.

Example:

A Summer Afternoon

Swish went the trees in the cool summer breeze
Splash-splish went the fish in the stream.
Crash-bang went the thunder, kerplop went the rain,
And woke me from my dream!

On your own: First, list echoic words on the lines below. Then, use some of these words in an echoic poem.

_____   _____

_____   _____

_____   _____

_____   _____

_____   _____

Name _____

Crazy Creature Poem

A **crazy creature poem** is one in which the poet describes an imaginary animal that possesses some of the features and exhibits some of the characteristics of two or more real animals. The title of a crazy creature poem is often created by combining parts of the names of these animals.

Example:

Duck-e-phant

He waddles when he walks
And he quacks when he talks,
But on the ground he'll have to stay.
He runs and jumps and flaps and falls,
'Cause his ears get in the way.

"How will I get from here to there?"
He cried and quacked and squawked.
"If my wings and ears don't soon make friends,
I'll just pack my trunk and walk!"

On your own: Combine the features of two or more different animals to make a one-of-a-kind creature. First, draw a picture of this creature on a separate sheet of paper. Next, write a humorous poem about this creature on the lines below. Finally, combine part or all of each animal's name to create a name for your created creature and a title for your poem.

_____

_____

_____

_____

_____

_____

_____

_____

_____

Name _____

Poetry Contract

Complete each project that has been marked.

Poetry Folder

☐ Write each of the different kinds of poems as it is assigned. Once a poem has been checked and returned to you, place it in your poetry folder.

☐ Select a theme and write it on the line below. Follow this theme when you write each of the different kinds of poems assigned to you. After each poem has been checked and returned to you, place it in your poetry folder. (**Possible themes:** animals, climates, countries, flowers, friendship, holidays, insects, school, sea creatures, seasons, sports, trees, etc.)

My theme is _____.

Poetry Appreciation

☐ Using poetry books, find five poems that you really enjoy reading. Copy them exactly as the author has written them. Include the title and the author's name. Keep them in your poetry folder.

☐ Using poetry books, find five poems that share the theme you have chosen. Copy them exactly as the author has written them. Include the title and the author's name. Keep them in your poetry folder.

Poetry Recitation

☐ Choose a poem from your collection to memorize. Be prepared to recite this poem to the class.

☐ Choose a poem from your collection to memorize. Record your poem on tape, being careful to include your name, the title of the poem, and the poet's name. While you are recording, speak clearly and with expression. You may wish to add background music or sound effects. Play your tape-recorded poem for the class.

Poetry Book

☐ Print your poems on the pages of the mini-book that appears on pages 39-48 in this book. Illustrate these poems and then bind the pages together, following the instructions on page 38.

☐ Using your choice of book size and shape, write and illustrate your poems on separate sheets of paper. Then, bind these sheets together, following the instructions on page 38.

Name _____

Poetry Projects

1. Poetry is written to be heard. Practice reading a selection of your favorite mood poems aloud. Choose poems that are humorous, sad, or scary, and read them in your best theatrical voice. When you are satisfied with your performance, read the poems into a microphone, and tape record them to share with a group of younger students. Don't forget to mention the title of each poem and the name of its author as you record it.

2. Work with other students to create a book of original poems written and illustrated by members of your class. Carefully print or type two or three of your best original poems on unlined white paper. Illustrate them appropriately. Ask several of your classmates to do the same. Collect these poems in a class poetry book. Design a cover and title page for this book. When the book is finished, make it available in your classroom or school library.

3. Choose a theme and challenge class members to address this theme in a variety of poetic forms. Display the results on an appropriately decorated bulletin board or wall.

4. Make a poetry idea box. Search through old magazines and newspapers for pictures or photographs that could inspire imaginative poetry. Mount the pictures on cardboard or tagboard, and file them in a decorated box. Make the box available in a classroom poetry corner.

5. Compose a partner poem. Write the first line of a couplet and ask a classmate to supply the second line. If you are successful, write some additional couplets or add another classmate to your poetry partnership and try a triolet.

Name _____

Poetry Collage

Use pictures and words to create a poetry collage. Choose your favorite poem from a published source for this project.

What you need:

- one sheet of unlined white paper
- a pen or a typewriter
- old magazines and/or catalogs
- scissors
- one large sheet of construction paper or tagboard for the background
- glue

What you do:

1. Print or type the poem neatly, along with its title and the name of its author, on unlined white paper.

2. Carefully trim off the excess paper around the poem.

3. Look through old magazines and catalogs to find pictures, words, and phrases that capture the feeling or meaning of the poem.

4. Cut out these pictures, words, and phrases.

5. Arrange these pictures, words, and phrases collage-style on the construction paper or tagboard, allowing them to overlap in ways that make your composition interesting.

6. When you are satisfied with the arrangement, glue the cutouts in place.

7. When the glue has dried, glue the poem in the center of the paper or board, atop some of the pictures, words, and phrases.

8. Share your collage with other students by posting it on a bulletin board or displaying it in your classroom poetry corner.

How to Bind the Mini-Book

1. Duplicate the pages of the mini book back-to-back in the same order as they are printed in this book.

2. Cut the duplicated pages in half horizontally, and stack them so that the right-hand pages are in numerical order.

3. Cut two pieces of colored construction paper the same size as the book paper ($5\frac{1}{2}'' \times 8\frac{1}{2}''$).

4. Fold the pages of the book in half.

5. Place the two sheets of construction paper back-to-back on the outside.

6. Using a sewing machine and a relatively long stitch, sew the book's pages and the construction paper sheets together, leaving at least 3″ of thread free at both the top and the bottom.

7. Tie the threads at both ends and clip off the excess thread close to the knots.

8. Cut two pieces of cardboard the size of your folded book plus $\frac{3}{8}''$ added to each dimension ($4\frac{5}{8}'' \times 5\frac{7}{8}''$).

9. Cut a large sheet of paper the size of your original unfolded pages plus 2″ in each dimension ($7\frac{1}{2}'' \times 10\frac{1}{2}''$).

10. Leaving a 1″ margin all the way around the paper, draw a cover illustration and print the title on the right-hand side of this sheet of paper.

11. Turn the cover over. Using rubber cement or glue, attach the two cardboard pieces to the inside of the cover so that they are centered on each side and are $\frac{3}{8}''$ apart in the middle.

12. Trim and miter the corners as shown.

13. Fold the paper edges over the cardboard, and rubber cement or glue them in place.

14. Place rubber cement or glue on the outside sheet of construction paper on your book, and carefully press your book against the inside of the cardboard cover.

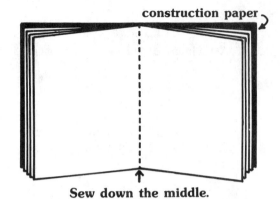

construction paper

Sew down the middle.

Draw a cover illustration and print the title on the right-hand side.

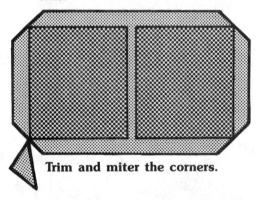

Trim and miter the corners.

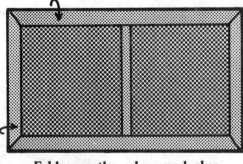

Fold over the edges and glue them in place.

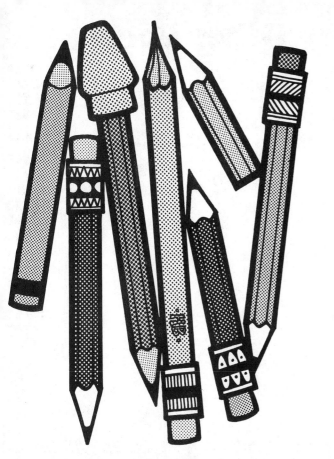

A Mini-Book
of Poetry

by

_____

F H T S A C C G N
E U K L Z W P D
B O J Q X M

My Favorite Poems

This book is
dedicated to

_____

35

Window Poem

Contrast Poem

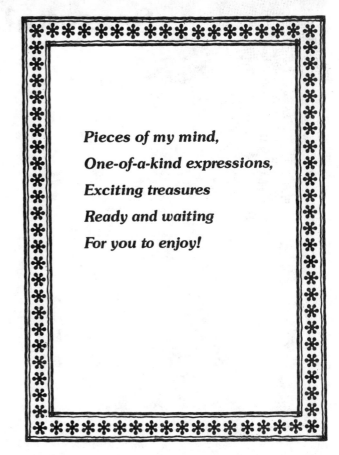

Pieces of my mind,
One-of-a-kind expressions,
Exciting treasures
Ready and waiting
For you to enjoy!

Creepy-Crawlies

Haiku

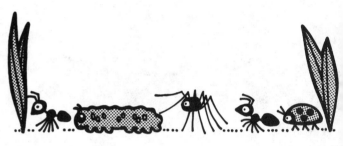

2

31

Five W's Poem

Triangular Triplet

Triangular Triplet

Five W's Poem

28

5

Triolet

Quinzaine

ABaAabAB & ABaAabAB

753753753753

Quinzaine

Triolet

✳753753753753✳

6

ABaAabAB & ABaAabAB

27

Acrostic Poem

Let's Get Lyrical

YKSJGZNO

Alliteration

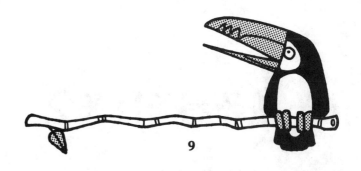

24

9

Echoic Poem

Greetings!

Cinquain

Echoic Poem

1✳4✳6✳8✳2

10

rrrrrrrrrrrrrrro

23

Crazy Creature Poems

Parody

Couplets

Comparisons

HH PP UU FF SS

20

13

Wish Poem

Diamante

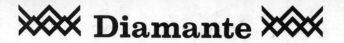 **Diamante**  **Wish Poem**

14

19

- -

Who's Who Clerihew